Wild Critters

Verse by Tim Jones • Photography by Tom Walker

Arctic fox pups

Co-published by:

Epicenter Press
Fairbanks / Seattle

Graphics Arts Center Publishing Co.
Portland, Oregon

Cover Design: Leslie Newman, Newman Design/Illustration
Inside Design: Tim Jones, Leslie Newman
Illustrations: Leslie Newman
Imagesetting: Thomas & Kennedy, Inc.
Printer: Palace Press
Editors: Ariell Adams Huff, Kent Sturgis

Copyright © 1992 by Tom Walker and Tim Jones. All rights reserved. No
part of this publication may be reproduced or transmitted in any form or
by any means, electronic or mechanical, without written permission of
the publisher.

This book, printed on acid-free paper, has been produced in conjunction
with Palace Press's Plant-a-Tree program in which approximately 11 trees
will be planted to replace those used in its manufacture.

Library of Congress Cataloging-in-Publication Data

Jones, Tim, 1942 –
    Wild Critters / Tim Jones.
        p. cm
    Summary: Photography of Alaskan wildlife is accompanied by
    humorous verses about the animals.
    ISBN 0-945397-11-9 (hard)

    1. Animals—Juvenile poetry. 2. Zoology—Alaska—Juvenile poetry.
3. Children's poetry, American. [1. Animals—Poetry. 2. Zoology—
Alaska—Poetry. 3. Humorous poetry.] I. Title.
PS3560.0547W55   1991
811' .54—dc20

91-7308
CIP

AC

Co-published by:

Epicenter Press Inc.
18821 64th Ave. N.E., Seattle, WA 98155 (206) 485-6822
P.O. Box 60529, Fairbanks, AK 99706 (907) 474-4969
and

Graphic Arts Center Publishing Co.
P.O. Box 10306, Portland, OR 97210 (503) 226-2402

Printed in Singapore through Palace Press of San Francisco

Wild Critters

White-front goose

Bald eagle

For Mary Anne, Justin, Ariel and Eric

With special thanks to:
Mary Lou Barra, Phil Barra, Jon Goniwiecha,
Barbara Jones, Dona Kubina, Penny Mathes,
Yeon Soon Min, Nita Pardovich, Gari Normand,
Evie Smith and Jim Swaney.

Tufted puffins

TABLE OF CONTENTS

The sound of silence 8

A yawn dawning. 10

Caribou Carrie 12

One stuck duck. 14

Back seat loonacy 16

The view forever. 18

Camouflage 20

Oh, for a hide to hide in. 22

Sea otter transit authority 24

The Arctic waterbed 26

Flower child 28

Poor George bear 30

Peekaboo caribou 32

Determined ermine 34

Pfine pfeathered pfashion 36

The terrible twos 38

Snorkeling 40

Cooling your wheels 42

Cool courage 44

Whatever can a walrus do? 46

The sound of silence

8

In the spring
on the wing
you can hear
the geese sing.

In the fall
in a squall
you can still
hear them call.

On the ground
there's no sound
they don't want
to be found.

Snow geese

Canada goose

A yawn dawning

Midnight sun
sounds like fun,
until you hunt all day.

With all that light
there's not much night,
to sleep fatigue away.

With only dusk 'til dawning
I always wake up yawning
to start my new foray.

Red fox

Caribou Carrie

Caribou Carrie
stretched for a berry
and caught it up in her rack.

She reached for the treat,
fell off her feet
and tied a knot in her back.

Caribou

One stuck duck

Dipper duck
ran out of luck
and got his head stuck
in the muck.

Female mallard duck tipping up to feed

Back seat loonacy

Are we there yet, are we there yet?
Cried the little loon.
No we are not there yet,
but we will be there soon.

Are we there yet, are we there yet?
Cried the little loon.
No we are not there yet,
why don't we sing a tune?

Are we there yet, are we there yet?
Still the same old beat.
No we are not there yet,
why don't you try to eat?

Are we there yet, are we there yet?
Her call was still the same.
No we are not there yet,
why don't you play a game?

Are we there yet, are we there yet?
She called out with a yap.
No we are not there yet,
why don't you take a nap?

Are we there yet, are we there yet?
We better get there quick,
if you don't stop this moving—
I am going to get sick.

Are we there yet, are we there yet?
Cried the little loon.
No, my little darling,
but we will be there soon.

16

Common loon and her chick

The view forever

Mama takes me up these hills
but never far enough
for me to see around and over
every rock and bluff.

So when I can't see all there is
and want to see whatever,
I climb a little higher
and I can see forever.

Dall sheep

Camouflage

Camouflage, camouflage,
such a silly word,
three little syllables
sounding so absurd.

But in the woods
it means a lot
and makes me hard to get.
Camouflage, camouflage,
can you see me yet?

Willow ptarmigan in winter and summer plumage

Oh, for a hide to hide in

It's fun to be a different moose
and wear an all-white gown.
I can go to moose's parties,
act like quite a clown.

But, white I can be spied in
and when hunters come around,
I'd like a darker hide to hide in,
maybe something in plain brown.

White moose

Sea otter transit authority

Otter ran a ferry trip
from here to over there.
Anyone could ride along
if they paid the fare.

Snow crab asked to take a ride,
to see his buddy bunch.
Climb aboard, the otter said,
we'll even do some lunch.

Sea otter and snow crabs

The Arctic waterbed

White bear wanders polar cap
with no rhyme to his heading,
looking for a place to nap,
a place with good soft bedding.

He finds a spot along his hike,
a bed that will suffice,
a comfy place a bear would like,
a nice, white sheet of ice.

Polar bear sleeping

Flower child

I don't do what others do
and some think I'm a snob.
I prefer my fields of flowers
to the madding mob.

Few can understand me
and some say I'm a slob.
All they do is tell me,
"Get a haircut, get a job."

Musk ox

Poor George bear

Old George bear,
big George bear,
how will you ever
comb your hair?

On a stump,
on a tree,
on a sign you see.

Grizzly bear

Peekaboo caribou

The tundra hasn't anything
that's tall of which to speak;
nothing big to hide behind
when playing hide and seek.

With nowhere else to go
to hide from one another,
I found the safest place to hide
is right behind my mother.

Caribou

Determined ermine

An ermine
in his winter whites
climbed a tree
to see the sights
and get himself
above the snow
that lay so deep
he couldn't go.

Too bad it was
a little twig
and couldn't hold
a thing that big.
It broke when ermine
made a shift
and sent him swimming
in a drift.

34

Least weasel (ermine)

Pfine pfeathered pfashion

Ptarmigan's a natty dresser,
planning plumage with panache.
In winter white's his fashion;
in summer brown's the catch.
In spring he can't make up his mind
and dresses mix and match.

Willow ptarmigan in early spring plumage

The terrible twos

Oh, cubs of mine, oh cubs of mine,
to grow up strong and sound
and be a bear you have to walk
with four feet on the ground.

But, Mama dear, oh Mama dear,
aren't bears allowed to choose
if they want to run on fours
or walk around on twos?

Oh cubs of mine, oh cubs of mine,
grow up to be fine ones.
But you can't be a bear at all
while standing on your hind ones.

But Mama dear, oh Mama dear,
to get food to our jaws,
we have to stretch and reach up high
and stand on our hind paws.

Oh cubs of mine, oh cubs of mine,
to grow you have to eat.
But you won't grow to be a bear
while standing on two feet.

But, Mama dear, oh Mama dear,
if berries we're to find,
we have to walk on twos to see
round Mama's big behind.

Female grizzly bear and her cubs

Snorkeling

When they put these ponds around,
they should warn us, I contend,
to tell us where it's shallow
and how to miss the deep end.

Moose

Cooling your wheels

A snowshoe hare
with racing flair
went hopping 'cross the fields.

The snowshoe hare
with hair to spare
got snow caught in his heels.

The snowshoe hare,
befuddled there,
stopped to clean his wheels.

Snowshoe hare

Cool courage

I've stood upon the high rocks
while my muscles twitch and quiver,
as I try to build my courage
to jump into the river.

But just when I'm about to go,
a hot dog blows my hero's dream
and makes me look a coward
as he goes and jumps upstream.

44

Brown bear and salmon

Whatever can a walrus do?

When I get scared deep in the night
of monsters in the gloom,
I pull the covers way up tight
to chase them from the room.

Whatever can a walrus do
when facing such a fright,
out there lying on the sand
no hiding place in sight?

Pacific walrus

Barbara Jones photo

Tom Walker has lived in Alaska for more than 20 years and during most of that time he has been involved somehow with the state's wild critters. He worked as a technician with the Alaska Department of Fish and Game and as a wilderness guide until he found his true calling as a writer and photographer of Alaska's wonderful wildlife. Since 1970 he has traveled to and lived in some of the most remote parts of Alaska recording the sights and thoughts of a wildnerness hand and brought those images to a world of readers who might otherwise only imagine what exists out beyond the horizon. He has written three books, *We Live in the Alaskan Bush*, *Building the Alaska Log Home* and, most recently, *Shadows on the Tundra*. A fourth book, *Alaskan Wildlife,* is filled with his photographs of Alaska animals. His wildlife images have appeared in a number of national magazines including National Geographic, National Wildlife, Natural History and Audubon and to date his photos have graced 27 magazine covers.

Tim Jones moved to Alaska in 1973 and worked several years at the Anchorage Daily News and Alaska Magazine. In 1980 he left the confines of Anchorage for broader horizons becoming a boat captain in Prince William Sound, a sometime commercial fisherman, and built his own cabin in the Alaska Bush, incidentally using Tom Walker's book as a guide. He is the author of *The Last Great Race* and co-author of *Race Across Alaska*, two books about Alaska's 1,000-plus mile Iditarod Trail Sled Dog Race. He has edited several books about Alaska. His magazine credits include Alaska Magazine, We Alaskans, The Alaska Journal, Sports Illustrated, Anna's House and Cruising World. He is now working as a coordinator for fishing vessels that might be called out in the event of another oil spill in Prince William Sound. He writes as he finds the time.